PRESIDENTIAL (Mis)SPEAK
The Very Curious Language of George W. Bush™

Volume 1

Edited by

Robert S. Brown

★ ★ ★ ★

Outland Books
Outland Communications, LLC
Skaneateles, New York

For information about discount purchases or purchasing Outland's George W. Bush
Desk Calendars, please contact Outland Books at (315) 685-8723 or www.outlandbooks.com

Published by Outland Books
Outland Communications, LLC
P.O. Box 534
25 Hannum Street
Skaneateles, New York 13152

www.outlandbooks.com

ISBN: 0-9714102-3-2

Design by HumanDesign

Printed in the United States of America

To Joni and our girls,
Timree, Laura, Elizabeth, Emily, Robin and Alex.
Without your loving patience and support
this book could never have been completed.

*"For every fatal shooting, there were roughly three
non-fatal shootings. And, folks, this is unacceptable
in America. It's just unacceptable.
And we're going to do something about it."*
George W. Bush

*"People make suggestions on what to say all the time.
I'll give you an example. I don't read what's handed
to me. People say; 'Here, here's your speech,' or
'Here's an idea for a speech.' They're changed. Trust me."*
George W. Bush

INTRODUCTION

I'm thinking of editing a book on rock gardens or butterfly collections or maybe home remedies for the common cold. Anything that has nothing to do with the "new" political correctness or presidential approval ratings. A publishing venture that is insulated from the ravages of war, terrorism, death, and destruction... Maybe a book on sex. That should retain its viability in the marketplace come hell or nucular annihilation. All right then, sex will be the next project. I'll just have to figure a way to keep it from my daughters and our entire community. I just won't tell any of them.

If you want to test your reserves and find out who your friends really are, especially within your extended family, edit a desk calendar and then a book, both on George W. Bush's peculiar oratorical stylings, and set your timing as follows. Arrange for your 2002 Desk Calendar to go to print on September 12, 2001. And then, if you're feeling up to it, choose to release the calendar's paperback book version during the first week of the War on Iraq—just as the first casualty figures are beginning to sink in.

What else can I do for fun? I'm just not sure yet. Find out in the Introduction to Volume 2 of this series just how bad things can eventually get. Perhaps I'll just hold back release of the next volume until something especially sobering happens. Maybe I'll wait until that Presidential pretzel, by some horrific turn of fate, isn't actually coughed back up. That's when I'll make my move. Perfect timing. Sympathy will be running sky high. Bring out Volume 2.

I have an older brother who has always operated on the premise that whenever talking about something serious, one should act and be serious. So, being the wise-ass younger brother I've gone to some effort to develop a counter approach—just to be annoying. Actually, the first draft of this introduction was ever so serious and, accordingly, just didn't feel right. So I decided to fall back on the 'gonzo' journalism I first came upon in the mid 1970s when I read Hunter S. Thompson's *Fear and Loathing in Las Vegas* (still my favorite book title). The style felt reckless and liberating, especially since I came from a family of restrained, well-spoken, Harvard-educated men whose speech was always measured and in control. Well, I digress and am in real need of an editor here...

So, for the sake of my brother, seriously.

I have two requests. First, I would ask the 'gatekeepers' to allow for the free flow of thoughts and ideas. Don't let the events of September 11, 2001, frighten you into curbing the unrestrained discourse that has defined our freedom and liberty for over 200 years. You gatekeepers know who you are. For the rest of us, they are the publishers, retailers, buyers, sales representatives, and media outlets—together, the complicated apparatus that makes many decisions on our behalf. Which books, movies, art, ideas will we be exposed to? They decide. Give it all to us, and you might be surprised at our reaction. We are not the frightened, cowering, one-dimensional creatures you, at times, apparently think we are. We're stronger than that, we're more resilient than that, and we're more complex than that. Make available those things you think might offend us, and, in fact, some of us might take offense. But, that's okay, isn't it?

Second, to the mainstream American news media. I would only ask that you operate outside the box a little bit more. Why is it that when I'm interviewed by the Canadian or British, or Irish media, the U.S. President's communication style is seen as "newsworthy", but not so by you? The BBC and CBC query the significance associated with the fact that the American President appears to have only limited and confused access to the English vocabulary. Media exploration of this fine detail in the U.S. is left to the cast of Saturday Night Live. And, for example, are we really supposed to gloss over evidence that the sitting American President seems to misunderstand the separation of powers in the government that he leads? ("The legislature's job is to write law. It's the executive branch's job to interpret law.")

Further, one has only to travel outside the U.S. to fully appreciate the fear and trepidation felt all over the world, not because of this President's fairly astounding propensity to malaprop (I just made up that verb), but rather, his strident manner that would appear to be isolating our country more and more with each passing Presidential dictate fired off to the rest of the known world.

Well, I suppose the world will just have to get used to it because, as a White House official put it:

"That's how the President speaks."

RSB

"The education issue ought to be discussed about."

December 15, 2000   Speaking to press during a meeting with Louisiana Senator John Breaux in Austin, Texas.

"It is clear our nation is reliant upon big foreign oil. More and more of our imports come from overseas."

September 25, 2000   From a campaign speech delivered in Beaverton, Oregon.

"… Magna Carter…"

Circa May 30, 2001   Standing before giant redwood trees in California, the President stated that the trees were there when the "Magna Carter" was signed.

"Rarely is the question asked: Is our children learning?"

January 11, 2000 From a speech delivered in Florence, South Carolina, and as reported in the *Los Angeles Times* on January 14, 2000.

Reporter: "The European Union and Japan have filed a challenge in the WTO (World Trade Organization) against a rule in the Agriculture Appropriations bill that would allow steel companies to receive money from antidumping duties."

Bush: "Say again now?"

December 22, 2000 Spoken during a press conference held by the President-Elect.

"On election night we won. And then there was a recount, and we won. And there was a selected recount as a result of different legal maneuverings, and we won that. And I believe one of these days that all this is going to stop, and Dick Cheney and I will be the President and the Vice President."

November 30, 2000 Comment made during a campaign press conference.

★ ★ ★ ★

"They misunderestimated me."

November 6, 2000 Comment made in Bentonville, Arkansas.

★ ★ ★ ★

"Actually, this may sound a little West Texan to you, but I like it when I'm talking about myself, and when he's talking about myself, all of us are talking about me."

May 31, 2000 Spoken to Chris Matthews on MSNBC's *Hardball*.

"The important question is: How many hands have I shaked?"

October 23, 1999 Quoted by *The New York Times*. This was candidate Bush's response to a question about why he hadn't spent more time in New Hampshire.

"I understand small business growth. I was one."

February 19, 2000 Quoted in the *New York Daily News.*

"The Bob Jones policy on interracial dating, I mean I spoke out on interracial dating. I spoke out against that. I spoke out against interracial dating. I mean, I support inter—the policy of interracial dating."

February 25, 2000 Candidate Bush was referring to the official policies of Bob Jones University. From a CBS News broadcast.

"I think we agree, the past is over."

May 10, 2000 The Governor's comment after a meeting with Senator John McCain. Quoted in *The Dallas Morning News.*

PRESIDENTIAL (Mis)SPEAK

"What I am against is quotas. I am against hard quotas. Quotas, they basically delineate based upon whatever. However they delineate, quotas, I think, vulcanize society. So, I don't know how that fits into what everybody else is saying—their relative positions—but that's my position."

January 21, 2000 Quoted in the *San Francisco Chronicle*.

"We ought to make the pie higher."

February 15, 2000 Comment made in Columbia, South Carolina, during presidential campaign.

"I think if you say you're going to do something and don't do it, that's trustworthiness."

August 30, 2000 From a CNN online chat.

"I don't want to win? If that were the case, why the heck am I on the bus 16 hours a day, shaking thousands of hands, giving hundreds of speeches, getting pillared in the press and cartoons and still staying on message to win?"

February 28, 2000 Quoted in *Newsweek* magazine.

PRESIDENTIAL (Mis)SPEAK

"It's good to see so many friends here in the Rose Garden. This is our first event in this beautiful spot, and it's appropriate we talk about policy that will affect people's lives in a positive way in such a beautiful, beautiful park of our national—really, our national park system, my guess is you would want to call it."

February 8, 2001   Address to a gathering in the Rose Garden at the White House.

"Keep good relations with the Grecians."

June 12, 1999   As quoted in *The Economist*.

PRESIDENTIAL (Mis)SPEAK

"I know how hard it is for you to put food on your family."

January 27, 2000   During a campaign speech in Nashua, New Hampshire.

"I've changed my style somewhat, as you know. I'm less, I pontificate less, although it may be hard to tell it from this show. And I'm more interacting with people."

February 13, 2000   From NBC's *Meet the Press*.

"Uh, I support winning."

April 7, 1999   Spoken on CNN's *Inside Politics*. Referring to America's involvement in Kosovo.

"Put the off button on."

February 14, 2000   Advice to parents who have concerns about violence on television.

Reporter: "A question for both of you. There's been a lot said about how different you are as people. Have you already, in your talks, found something maybe that you—some personal interests that you have in common, maybe in religion or sport or music?"

Bush: "We both use Colgate toothpaste."

February 23, 2001   From a joint press conference held at Camp David with British Prime Minister Tony Blair.

PRESIDENTIAL (Mis)SPEAK

"Whatever it took to help Taiwan defend theirself."

April 25, 2001 Speaking on ABC's *Good Morning America*. Describing the United States' commitment to the defense of Taiwan.

"The Senator [John McCain] has got to understand if he's going to have— he can't have it both ways. He can't take the high horse and then claim the low road."

February 17, 2000 From a campaign speech in Florence, South Carolina.

"Well, it's an unimaginable honor to be the President during the Fourth of July of this country. It means what these words say, for starters. The great inalienable rights of our country. We're blessed with such values in America. And I—it's—I'm a proud man to be the nation based upon such wonderful values."

July 2, 2001 Spoken during a visit to the Jefferson Memorial in Washington, D.C.

"Neither in French, nor in English, nor in Mexican."

April 21, 2001 The President's response when asked if he would answer a reporter's question. Summit of the Americas, Quebec City, Canada.

"Anyway, I'm so thankful, and so gracious. I'm gracious that my brother Jeb is concerned about the hemisphere as well."

June 4, 2001 During a visit to Miami and while appearing with his brother, Jeb, the Governor of Florida.

Bush: "I talked to my little brother, Jeb—I haven't told this to many people, but he's the Governor of—I shouldn't call him my little brother—my brother, Jeb, the great Governor of Texas."

Interviewer: "Florida."

Bush: "Florida. The state of the Florida."

April 27, 2000 Interview with Jim Lehrer of *The NewsHour with Jim Lehrer*.

"The person who runs FEMA [Federal Emergency Management Agency] is someone who must have the trust of the President because the person who runs FEMA really is the first voice oftentimes that someone whose lives have been turned upside down hears from."

January 4, 2001   Comment made at a press conference.

"Quotas are bad for America. It's not the way America is all about."

October 18, 2000   Spoken in St. Louis, Missouri.

"Laura and I really don't realize how bright our children is sometimes until we get an objective analysis."

April 15, 2000 Comment made on NBC's *Meet the Press.*

"For every fatal shooting, there were roughly three non-fatal shootings. And, folks, this is unacceptable in America. It's just unacceptable. And we're going to do something about it."

May 14, 2001

PRESIDENTIAL (Mis)SPEAK

Reporter: "Mr. President…"

Bush: "Speak clearly."

Reporter: "I'll try, sir. It's one of the things I have problems with."

Bush: "Speak for yourself."

June 12, 2001   Press conference with President Aznar of Spain in Madrid.

"This is Preservation Month. I appreciate preservation. It's what you do when you run for President. You gotta preserve."

Circa January 28, 2000   Candidate Bush was referring to **Perseverance** Month during a speech at Fairgrounds Elementary School in Nashua, New Hampshire. He was quoted in the January 28 issue of the *Los Angeles Times*.

"Reading is the basics for all learning."

March 28, 2000 Comment from a campaign stop in Reston, Virginia. The candidate was announcing his "Reading First" initiative.

★ ★ ★ ★

Larry King: [Vice President Gore said that] "If you lopped off the top 1% that you are giving tax relief... you could pay for the cost of every other program."

Bush: "Oh, I don't—you know, I hadn't—I'm not so sure. I'm not quick in my mind at math, but I don't believe in trying to pick and choose winners when it comes to tax relief."

September 26, 2000 Appearing on CNN's *Larry King Live*.

"We respect the other person. We always don't agree, but we respect, and we tolerate."

July 23, 2002 Speaking at the Argonne National Laboratory in Argonne, Illinois.

"I would have to ask the questioner. I haven't had a chance to ask the questioners the question they've been questioning. On the other hand, I firmly believe she'll be a fine Secretary of Labor. And I've got confidence in Linda Chavez. She is a—she'll bring an interesting perspective to the Labor Department."

January 8, 2001 Austin, Texas.

PRESIDENTIAL (Mis)SPEAK

"The way I like to put it is this: There's no bigger issue for the President to remind the moms and dads of America, if you happen to have a child, be fortunate to have a child."

March 16, 2001   Speaking to employees of the U.S. Treasury Department.

"This case has had full analyzation and has been looked at a lot. I understand the emotionality of death penalty cases."

June 23, 2000   Quoted in the Seattle *Post-Intelligencer*.

"I'm also honored to be here with the Speaker of the House—just happens to be from the state of Illinois. I'd like to describe the Speaker as a trustworthy man. He's the kind of fellow who says when he gives you his word he means it. Sometimes that doesn't happen all the time in the political process."

March 6, 2001   Speaking in Chicago, Illinois.

"Our priorities is our faith."

October 10, 2000   From a campaign speech in Greensboro, North Carolina.

"I suspect that had my dad not been President, he'd be asking the same questions: How'd your meeting go with so-and-so? How did you feel when you stood up in front of the people for the State of the Union Address—State of the Budget Address—whatever you call it?"

March 9, 2001   From an interview with *The Washington Post.*

"It's going to require numerous IRA agents."

October 10, 2000   The presidential candidate commenting on Vice President Gore's proposed tax plan (meaning to say IRS—Internal Revenue Service—agents).

PRESIDENTIAL (Mis)SPEAK

"If the terriers and bariffs are torn down, this economy will grow."

January 7, 2000   Spoken in Rochester, New York, during the presidential campaign.

"I assured the prime minister my administration will work hard to lay the foundation of peace in the Middle—to work with our nations in the Middle East, give peace a chance. Secondly, I told him that our nation will not try to force peace, that we'll facilitate peace and that we will work with those responsible for a peace."

March 20, 2001   Speaking with the press at the White House during a meeting with Ariel Sharon.

PRESIDENTIAL (Mis)SPEAK

"We cannot let terrorists and rogue nations hold this nation hostile or hold our allies hostile."

August 21, 2000   Comments from a campaign speech delivered in Des Moines, Iowa.

"Putting Education First."

July 2000   George W. Bush's Presidential Campaign website
The presidential candidate's website gave a priority ranking to important issues of concern to the Governor. "Putting Education First" was ranked No. 3 on the list.

"I want to reduce our own nucular capacities to the level commiserate with keeping the peace."

October 23, 2000   Spoken in Des Moines, Iowa, during a campaign address.

The Very Curious Language of George W. Bush™
Volume 1

"Drug therapies are replacing a lot of medicines as we used to know it."

October 17, 2000   Comments from a St. Louis, Missouri, presidential debate.

"They said, 'You know, this issue doesn't seem to resignate with the people.' And I said, 'You know something? Whether it resignates or not doesn't matter to me because I stand for doing what's the right thing.'"

October 31, 2000   Quoted in *Slate* magazine—from comments made in Portland, Oregon.

PRESIDENTIAL (Mis)SPEAK

"That's a chapter, the last chapter of the twentieth, twentieth, twenty-first century that most of us would rather forget. The last chapter of the twentieth century. This is the first chapter of the twenty-first century."

October 24, 2000   Comment made by the presidential candidate in Arlington Heights, Illinois.

"I know the human being and fish can coexist peacefully."

September 29, 2000   Comment made in Saginaw, Michigan, during the presidential campaign.

"The administration I'll bring is a group of men and women who are focused on what's best for America—honest men and women, decent men and women, women who will see service to our country as a great privilege and who will not stain the house."

January 15, 2000   Spoken during the Republican debate in Des Moines, Iowa.

"It's kinda jungley."

August 25, 2001   Referring to a trail he is clearing on his Crawford, Texas, ranch.

"That woman who knew I had dyslexia; I never interviewed her."

Circa September 16, 2000   The presidential candidate is referring to Gail Sheehy, who had written an article for *Vanity Fair*, proposing that Governor Bush suffered from dyslexia.

Interviewer: "So, tell me again why Crawford is such a great vacation spot? I mean, most people would think…"

Bush: "Well it's my home. If you're a home person, a person who appreciates home, then you understand what I'm trying to say."

August 10, 2001   Being interviewed by an ABC News correspondent while on vacation at his ranch in Crawford, Texas.

PRESIDENTIAL (Mis)SPEAK

"There are some monuments where the land is so widespread, they just encompass as much as possible. And the integral part of the—the precious part, so to speak—I guess all land is precious, but the part that the people uniformly would not want to spoil, will not be despoiled."

March 13, 2001   Comment made while speaking to the press—Washington, D.C.

"It's about past seven in the evening here, so we're actually in different time lines."

January 30, 2001   The President was speaking to Philippine President Gloria Macapagal Arroyos. He was in Washington, D.C., she was in Manila. As reported by *The New York Times*.

"The fundamental question is: 'Will I be a successful President when it comes to foreign policy?' I will be, but, until I'm the President, it's going to be hard for me to verify that I think I'll be more effective."

June 27, 2000 Comment made in Wayne, Michigan, during the presidential campaign.

"That's how the President speaks."

White House official March 8, 2001 Referring to the fact that the President had used a "present" verb tense when he had intended to use the "future" tense (in reference to U.S. agreements with North Korea). Quoted in *The New York Times*.

"We spent a lot of time talking about Africa, as we should. Africa is a nation that suffers from incredible disease."

June 14, 2001   From comments made in Gothenburg, Sweden.

"The role of government is to create an environment that encourages Hispanic-owned businesses, women-owned businesses, anybody-kind-of-owned businesses."

March 19, 2001

PRESIDENTIAL (Mis)SPEAK

"I want to thank you for coming to the White House to give me an opportunity to urge you to work with these five senators and three congressmen, to work hard to get this trade promotion authority moving. The power that be, well most of the power that be, sits right here."

June 18, 2001 Washington, D.C.

"A tax cut is really one of the anecdotes to coming out of an economic illness."

September 18, 2000 Spoken while a guest on the CBS show, *The Edge With Paula Zahn.*

The Very Curious Language of George W. Bush™
Volume 1

"It's very important for folks to understand that when there's more trade there's more commerce."

April 21, 2001   From comments made in Quebec City, Canada.

"For those that are uninsured, many of the uninsured are able-bodied, capable people, capable of buying insurance, choose not to do so."

November 10, 1999   Comments made during an interview with *WMUR* in Manchester, New Hampshire.

"In terms of being a President that says there's no place in racism, it starts with saying there's no place for racism in America..."

January 10, 2000   Spoken during a Republican debate held in Michigan.

★ ★ ★ ★

"If you're sick and tired of the politics of cynicism and polls and principles, come and join this campaign."

February 16, 2000   Speaking at Hilton Head, South Carolina, during the presidential campaign.

★ ★ ★ ★

"It's your money. You paid for it."

October 18, 2000 Comment made in La Crosse, Wisconsin.

"We want our teachers to be trained so they can meet the obligations— their obligations as teachers. We want them to know how to teach the science of reading, in order to make sure there's not this kind of federal cufflink."

March 30, 2000 During a campaign stop at the Fritsche Middle School in Milwaukee, Wisconsin.

"I do remain confident in Linda [Chavez]. She'll make a fine Labor Secretary. From what I've read in the press accounts, she's perfectly qualified."

January 8, 2001 Comment by the President-Elect during a press conference.

"This is still a dangerous world. It's a world of madmen and uncertainty and potential mential losses."

January 14, 2000 Quoted in the *Financial Times*.

Reporter: "I have a three-part question for you, Mr. President, and a one-part question for you, Prime Minister Blair."

Bush: "Well, wait a minute, that's four questions."

Reporter: "Oh no, it's just actually one question."

Bush: "OK, good."

Reporter: "… in three parts."

Bush: "I see."

July 19, 2001   From official "10 Downing St." transcript of a press conference with President Bush and British Prime Minister Tony Blair.

"The point is, is that I want America to lead the nation—lead the world—toward a more safe world when it comes to nucular weaponry."

January 27, 2000   Quoted in *The New York Times.*

"I don't think we need to be subliminable about the differences between our views on prescription drugs."

September 12, 2000   Quoted by *Slate* magazine from comments made in Orlando, Florida.

"Really proud of it. A great campaign. And I'm really pleased with the organization and the thousands of South Carolinians that worked on my behalf. And I'm very gracious and humbled."

February 20, 2000

"The legislature's job is to write law. It's the executive branch's job to interpret law."

November 22, 2000 Comment made in Austin, Texas, and reported by *Slate* magazine.

"I'm gonna talk about the ideal world, Chris. I've read—I understand reality. If you're asking me as the President, would I understand reality, I do."

May 31, 2000 Governor Bush answering a question from Chris Matthews on MSNBC's *Hardball*.

"I don't remember any kind of heaviness ruining my time at Yale."

Quote from *Favorite Son* (page 117)—A reference to the 1960s Civil Rights movement.

"We need a full affront on an energy crisis that is real in California and looms for other parts of our country if we don't move quickly."

March 29, 2001   White House press conference.

"I'm pretty good about asking myself the own question, then answering it, see?"

May 31, 2000   Answering a question posed by Chris Matthews on MSNBC's *Hardball*.

"If affirmative action means what I just described, what I'm for, then I'm for it."

October 17, 2000 St. Louis, Missouri, presidential debate.

"Those of us who spent time in the agricultural sector and in the heartland, we understand how unfair the death penalty is—the death tax is. I don't want to get rid of the death penalty, just the death tax."

February 28, 2001

"I quit drinking in 1986 and haven't had a drop since then. And it wasn't because of a government program, by the way—in my particular case—because I had a higher call."

November 3, 2000   Reported by CNN. Comment made in West Allis, Wisconsin.

"I know what I believe. I will continue to articulate what I believe, and what I believe—I believe what I believe is right."

July 22, 2001   Comment made during a visit to Rome, Italy.

PRESIDENTIAL (Mis)SPEAK

"We have practically banished religious values and religious institutions from the public square and constructed a discountfort zone for even discussing our faith in public settings."

September 9, 2000 From a speech in Milwaukee, Wisconsin.

Ted Koppel: "So he's your lightning rod?"

Bush: "More than that, he's my sounding rod."

July 21, 2000 Referring to vice presidential candidate, Dick Cheney, on ABC's *Nightline*.

Reporter: [Do you have] "any take at all" [on Russian President Vladimir Putin?]

Bush: "I really don't. I will if I'm the President."

November 21, 1999   On NBC's *Meet the Press.*

"Do not subscribe—I mean, you know, you cannot subscribe those views to me…"

February 13, 2000   Comment made on NBC's *Meet the Press.* Mr. Bush was referring to whether or not he agreed with the views espoused by the chancellor of Bob Jones University.

"One reason I like to highlight reading is reading is the beginnings of the ability to be a good student. And if you can't read, it's going to be hard to realize dreams. It's going to be hard to go to college. So when your teachers say read—you ought to listen to her."

February 8, 2001

"I don't want nations feeling like that they can bully ourselves and our allies."

October 23, 2000   Comment made in Des Moines, Iowa.

"I don't have to accept their tenants. I was trying to convince those college students to accept my tenants. And I reject any labeling me because I happened to go to the university."

February 23, 2000 Referring to his visit to Bob Jones University.

"I mean, there needs to be a wholesale effort against racial profiling, which is illiterate children."

October 11, 2000 Comment made during a presidential debate.

PRESIDENTIAL (Mis)SPEAK

"The administration is doing everything we can to end the stalemate in an efficient way. We're making the right decisions to bring the solution to an end."

April 10, 2001 Washington, D.C.

"The fact that he relies on facts—says things that are not factual—are going to undermine his campaign."

March 4, 2000 Referring to Al Gore. Quoted in *The New York Times*.

"You saw the President yesterday. I thought he was very forward-leaning, as they say in diplomatic nuanced circles."

July 23, 2001   Referring to his meeting with President Vladimir Putin of Russia.

"If you don't stand for anything, you don't stand for anything. If you don't stand for something, you don't stand for anything."

November 2, 2000   Quoted by the *Austin American-Statesman*.

"I've supported the administration in Colombia. I think it's important for us to be training Colombians in that part of the world. The hemisphere is in our interest to have a peaceful Colombia."

October 11, 2000   Presidential debate—Winston-Salem, North Carolina.

"I'm sure there'll be moments when we don't agree 100% of the time."

December 2, 2000   Speaking to the press. Referring to the relationship between himself and Republican Congress.

Bush: "I look forward to future press conferences."

Reporter: "Frequently?"

Bush: "Well, yes, of course."

Reporter: "Once a week?"

Bush: "Oh, you don't want to see me once a week. You'll run out of questions."

Reporter: "You mean twice?"

Bush: "Oh, twice, I'll be running out of ties."

February 22, 2001   White House press conference.

★ ★ ★ ★

Reporter #1: "Mr. President —"

Reporter #2: "Mr. President, you gave me the floor."

Bush: "You're next. No, next to next. Let me rephrase it. You're last."

March 29, 2001   White House press conference.

"The great thing about America is everybody should vote."

December 8, 2000   Spoken in Austin, Texas.

"I don't care what the polls say. I don't. I'm doing what I think what's wrong."

March 15, 2000 The presidential candidate referring to his proposed economic plan—as reported in *The New York Times.*

"It's evolutionary, going from Governor to President, and this is a significant step, to be able to vote for yourself on the ballot, and I'll be able to do so next fall, I hope."

March 8, 2000 Quoted by the *Associated Press.*

"Everybody who pays taxes is going to get tax relief. If you take care of an elderly in your home, you're going to get the personal exemption increased."

October 17, 2000   At the third presidential debate—in answer to a question about his tax plan.

"I have a different vision of leadership. A leadership is someone who brings people together."

August 18, 2000

PRESIDENTIAL (Mis)SPEAK

"I also have picked a Secretary for Housing and Human Development— Mel Martinez from the state of Florida."

December 20, 2000   Announcing selection of a candidate for Secretary of the Department of Housing and **Urban** Development.

"Natural gas is hemispheric. I like to call it hemispheric in nature because it is a product that we can find in our neighborhoods."

December 20, 2000   Comment made in Austin, Texas.

"The key to foreign policy is to rely on reliance."

November 1, 2000   Quoted from *The Washington Post*.

★ ★ ★ ★

Reporter: "Well, you're a secular official…"

Bush: "I agree. I am a secular official."

Reporter: "And not a missionary?"

Bush: "Sir, on the air strikes in Iraq, the Pentagon is now saying that most of the bombs used in those strikes missed their targets."

February 23, 2001   Quoted in *The New York Times*.

"I was raised in the West. The west of Texas. It's pretty close to California. In more ways than Washington, D.C., is close to California."

April 7, 2000   During a presidential campaign stop in Los Angeles, California.

"Any time we've got any kind of inkling that somebody is thinking about doing something to an American and something to our homeland, you've just got to know we're moving on it to protect the United Nations Constitution, and at the same time, we're protecting you."

October 31, 2002   Aberdeen, South Dakota.

"I want each and every American to know for certain that I'm responsible for the decisions I make, and each of you are as well."

September 20, 2000 From *Live With Regis.*

"We'll let our friends be the peace-keepers and the great country called America will be the pacemakers."

September 6, 2000 Candidate Bush speaking in Houston, Texas.

"I do not believe we've put a guilty—
I mean innocent—person to death in
the state of Texas."

June 16, 2000   From National Public Radio's *All Things Considered.*

★ ★ ★ ★

"I don't know whether I'm going to
win or not. I think I am. I do know
I'm ready for the job. And if not, that's
just the way it goes."

August 21, 2000

★ ★ ★ ★

"He has certainly earned a reputation as a fantastic mayor, because the results speak for themselves. I mean, New York's a safer place for him to be."

May 18, 2000 Speaking on *The Edge with Paula Zahn* about New York City Mayor Rudolph Giuliani.

"She is a member of a labor union at one point."

January 2, 2001 The President-Elect, announcing Linda Chavez as his nomination to be Secretary of the Department of Labor.

"Let me put it to you this way, I am not a revengeful person."

December, 2000 From a *Time* magazine interview published in the December 25, 2000 issue.

"Listen, Al Gore is a very tough opponent. He is the incumbent. He represents the incumbency. And a challenger is somebody who generally comes from the pack and wins, if you're going to win. And that's where I'm coming from."

September 7, 2000   From comments made in Detroit, Michigan.

"I've got a record, a record that is conservative and a record that is compassionated."

March 2, 2000   As quoted by *The New York Times*.

"I told all four that there were going to be some times where we don't agree with each other. But that's OK. If this were a dictatorship, it'd be a heck of a lot easier—just as long as I'm the dictator."

December 18, 2000 Comment made during his first trip to Washington, D.C., after winning the presidency.

"Families is where our nation finds hope, where wings take dream."

October 18, 2000 During a visit to La Crosse, Wisconsin.

"I want it to be said that the Bush administration was a results-oriented administration, because I believe the results of focusing our attention and energy on teaching children to read and achieving an education system that's responsive to the child and to the parents, as opposed to mired in a system that refuses to change, will make America what we want it to be—a more literate county and a hopefuller country."

January 11, 2001   Washington, D.C.

"I will have a foreign-handed foreign policy."

September 27, 2000 Comment made in Redwood, California, during the presidential campaign.

"We got no better friend in that part of the world than the Philippines, and as the (Filipino) President said, there are a lot of proud Philippines living in America."

November 20, 2001 Speaking to reporters in the Oval Office during a visit from Philippine President Gloria Macapagal-Arroyo. Aired on CNN.

"But younger workers, in order to make sure the system exists tomorrow—younger workers ought to be able to take some of your own money and invest it in safe securities to get a better rate of return on that money."

October 11, 2000   Presidential debate in Winston-Salem, North Carolina.

"My pan plays down an unprecedented amount of our national debt."

February 27, 2001   From a speech concerning the proposed federal budget.

"I'm sure you can imagine it's an unimaginable honor to live here."

June 18, 2001 The President speaking at the White House to agriculture leaders.

"I've been talking to Vicente Fox, the new President of Mexico—I know him—to have gas and oil sent to the United States... so we'll not depend on foreign oil."

October 3, 2000

"Unfairly but truthfully, our party has been tagged as being against things. Anti-immigrant, for example. And we're not a party of anti-immigrants. Quite the opposite. We're a party that welcomes people."

July 1, 2000   Spoken while in Cleveland, Ohio.

"I think there is some methodology in my travels."

March 5, 2001   Speaking to the press in Washington, D.C.

"I would have said yes to abortion if only it was right. I mean, yeah, it's right. Well, no it's not right—that's why I said no to it."

February 14, 2000 Speaking in South Carolina.

"We must all hear the universal call to like your neighbor just like you like to be liked yourself."

January 14, 2000 Quoted in the *Financial Times*.

"But I also made it clear to [Russian President Vladimir Putin] that it's important to think beyond the old days of when we had the concept that if we blew each other up the world would be safe."

May 1, 2001 Speaking with reporters in Washington, D.C.

"Governor Bush will not stand for the subsidation of failure."

January 11, 2000 Quoted in the *New York Post*.

"I don't see many shades of gray in the war and terror. Either you're with us or you're against us. And it's a struggle between good and it's a struggle between evil."

February 8, 2002   Speaking in Denver, Colorado, at the 2002 Cattle Industry Annual Convention.

"For those who volunteered hour after hour to save a fellow citizens— somebody you didn't even know, but were willing to sacrifice on behalf of that citizen—thank you from grateful nation."

August 5, 2002   Speaking in Green Tree, Pennsylvania.

PRESIDENTIAL (Mis)SPEAK

"Redefining the role of the United States from enablers to keep the peace to enablers to keep the peace from peacekeepers is going to be an assignment."

January 14, 2001   Quoted in *The New York Times.*

"I don't feel like I've got all that much too important to say on the kind of big national issues."

September 15, 2000   Spoken on ABC's *20/20.*

The Very Curious Language of George W. Bush™
Volume 1

PRESIDENTIAL (Mis)SPEAK

"It's important for us to explain to our nation that life is important. It's not only life of babies, but it's life of children living in, you know, the dark dungeons of the Internet."

October 24, 2000 From a speech delivered in Arlington Heights, Illinois.

"Now, we talked to Joan Hanover. She and her husband, George, were visiting with us. They are near retirement—retiring—in the process of retiring—meaning they're very smart, active, capable people who are retirement age and are retiring."

February 12, 2003 Speaking in Alexandria, Virginia.

PRESIDENTIAL (Mis)SPEAK

"The government is not the surplus's money, Vice President."

November 5, 2000   From *The Washington Post.*

"A family in Allentown, Pennsylvania—I campaigned with them the other day… under my plan, they get $1,800 of tax relief. Under Vice President Gore's plan, they get $145 of tax relief. Now you tell me who stands on the side of the fence."

October 3, 2000   First presidential debate in Boston, Massachusetts.

PRESIDENTIAL (Mis)SPEAK

"We're beginning to change the way of thinking, so we ask the question; before we put you anywhere, we want to know what you know? And if you don't know what you're supposed to know, we'll correct it early before it's too late."

June 21, 2001 Speaking on education reform.

"I hope to get a sense of, should I be fortunate enough to be the President, how my administration will react to the Middle East."

October 12, 2000 From comments made in Winston-Salem, North Carolina.

PRESIDENTIAL (Mis)SPEAK

"I thought how proud I am to be standing up beside my dad. Never did it occur to me that he would become the gist for cartoonists."

February 28, 2000 Quoted in *Newsweek.*

"I am mindful not only of preserving executive powers for myself, but for predecessors as well."

January 29, 2001 Washington, D.C.

PRESIDENTIAL (Mis)SPEAK

"I mean, these good folks are revolutionizing how businesses conduct their business. And, like them, I am very optimistic about our position in the world and about its influence on the United States. We're concerned about the short term economic news, but long term I'm optimistic. And so, I hope investors hold investments for periods of time—that I've always found the best investments are those that you salt away based on economics."

January 4, 2001 Austin, Texas.

"There's nothing more than we'd like to do is to work with our friends to provide a humanitarian assistance…"

July 31, 2002 Referring to the Palestinian people during remarks at a photo opportunity with the Cabinet. White House, Washington, D.C.

"I support current efforts to make Amtrak more efficient and competitive. I believe these efforts will result in better, more extensive and more reliant rail service for the millions of Americans who travel by train."

September 17, 2000 Quoted by the *Associated Press.*

PRESIDENTIAL (Mis)SPEAK

"As I said in my State of the Union, liberty is not America's gift to the world. It is God's gift to human mankind, and that's what I believe."

February 12, 2003   Alexandria, Virginia.

"Those who think that they can say we're only going to have a stimulus package, but let's forget tax relief, misunderestimate—excuse me, underestimate (laughter)—just making sure you were paying attention. You were."

March 29, 2001   White House press conference.

The Very Curious Language of George W. Bush™
Volume 1

PRESIDENTIAL (Mis)SPEAK

Interviewer: "So, do you ever think about Al Gore?"

Bush: "Why? What do you mean?"

Interviewer: "Do you ever wonder what he's up to and think about last fall?"

Bush: "Not really."

August 10, 2001   Being interviewed by an ABC News correspondent at his ranch in Crawford, Texas.

"Home is important. It's important to have a home."

February 18, 2001   Comment made by the President in Crawford, Texas.

PRESIDENTIAL (Mis)SPEAK

"Dick Cheney and I do not want this nation to be in a recession. We want anybody who can find work to be able to find work."

December 5, 2000 Comment made on CBS's *60 Minutes II.*

"There is a lot of speculation and I guess there is going to continue to be a lot of speculation until the speculation ends."

October 18, 1998 The Texas Governor commenting on the possibility of his running for the presidency. Reported by the *Austin American-Statesman.*

PRESIDENTIAL (Mis)SPEAK

"Sometimes Churchill will talk back, sometimes he won't, depending upon the stress of the moment, but he is a constant reminder of what a great leader is like."

July 16, 2001   The President's assessment of the late Winston Churchill after receiving a bust of the former British Prime Minister from Tony Blair.

"Ann and I will carry out this equivocal message to the world. Markets must be open."

March 2, 2001   From the President's speech delivered during the swearing-in ceremony for Ann Veneman, the new Secretary of Agriculture.

The Very Curious Language of George W. Bush™
Volume 1

"If anybody harbors a terrorist, they're a terrorist. If they fund a terrorist, they're a terrorist. If they house terrorists, they're terrorists. I mean, I can't make it any more clearly to other nations around the world."

November 26, 2001 Answering questions from the press at the White House.

"I came away from that summit that the small business person feels constrained by tax policy and regulatory policy and I was really appreciated the people coming."

August 16, 2002 Speaking in Crawford, Texas.

"If you're asking me whether or not as to the innocence or guilt or if people have had adequate access to the courts in Texas, I believe they have."

June 10, 2000   Answer to a question posed by an *Associated Press* reporter.

"As Governor of Texas, I have set high standards for our public schools, and I have met those standards."

August 30, 2000   From the CNN Internet chat line.

"This is what I'm good at. I like meeting people, my fellow citizens. I like interfacing with them."

September 8, 2000   Comment made at a campaign stop in Pittsburgh, Pennsylvania.

"Laura and I are proud to call John and Michelle Engler our friends. I know you're proud to call him Governor. What a good man the Englers are."

November 3, 2000   From a speech made in Grand Rapids, Michigan.

"Kosovians can move back in."

April 9, 1999   Referring to the situation in Kosovo. CNN's *Inside Politics.*

"I've coined new words, like misunderstanding and Hispanically."

March 29, 2001   From a speech given at the Radio and Television Correspondents Association dinner in Washington, D.C.

"We're concerned about AIDS inside our White House. Make no mistake about it."

February 7, 2001   Washington, D.C.

"I wish I could turn to the soldiers on that ship, and I wish they could hear me. Stay in the military, there's a new commander-in-chief coming."

August 13, 2000   The presidential candidate was referring to the **sailors** stationed on an aircraft carrier anchored nearby.

"Now, by the way, surplus means a little money left over, otherwise it wouldn't be called a surplus."

October 27, 2000   From a campaign speech in Kalamazoo, Michigan.

"I hope we get to the bottom of the answer. It's what I'm interested to know."

April 26, 2000 The presidential candidate is referring to the Elian Gonzalez negotiations.

"There is book smart and the kind of smart that helps do calculus. But smart is also instinct and judgment and common sense. Smart comes in all kinds of different ways."

September 19, 2000 From a CNN interview.

"Well, they asked me of whether or not I'd meet with them."

December 16, 1999 In response to a question from Larry King, who inquired if the Governor had been asked to speak to a gay Republican group. From CNN's *Larry King Live.*

"The only thing I know about Slovakia is what I learned firsthand from your foreign minister, who came to Texas."

June 22, 1999 Governor Bush was referring to his meeting with the Prime Minister of Slovenia (Janez Drnovsek). Comment made to a Slovak journalist. Reported by the *Knight Ridder News Service.*

"The reason we start a war is to fight a war, win a war, thereby causing no more war."

October 3, 2000 Boston, Massachusetts. First presidential debate.

"Will the highways on the Internet become more few?"

January 29, 2000 Question asked by the candidate in Concord, New Hampshire, and reported in *Slate* magazine.

"Russia is no longer our enemy, and therefore we shouldn't be locked into a Cold War mentality that says we keep the peace by blowing each other up. In my attitude, that's old, that's tired, that's stale."

June 8, 2001 From a speech in Des Moines, Iowa.

"It's clearly a budget. It's got a lot of numbers in it."

May 5, 2000   Reported by *Reuters.*

"I mentioned early on that I recognize there are hurdles, and we're going to achieve those hurdles."

January 22, 2003   Speaking in St. Louis, Missouri.

"There is madmen in the world, and there are terror."

February 14, 2000   Comment reported by the *Associated Press.*

"Laura and I are looking forward to having a private dinner with he and Mrs. Blair Friday night."

February 22, 2001   Referring to the impending visit by British Prime Minister Tony Blair. White House press conference.

"My opponent keeps saying I give too much tax relief to the top 1%, but he hadn't heard my latest proposal. The bottom 99% will do well when they get to split Dick Cheney's stock options."

October 19, 2000   Joke delivered at the Al Smith Memorial Dinner in New York.

PRESIDENTIAL (Mis)SPEAK

"I think it's important for those of us in a position of responsibility to be firm in sharing our experiences, to understand that the babies out of wedlock is a very difficult chore for mom and baby alike... I believe we ought to say there is a different alternative than the culture that is proposed by people like Miss Wolf in society... And, you know, hopefully, condoms will work, but it hasn't worked."

November 21, 1999   From an appearance on NBC's *Meet the Press.*

PRESIDENTIAL (Mis)SPEAK

"There are some times when a President shows up that can make a situation worse, and, you know, I'm adverse to a camera. On the other hand, I think the President can either help or not help a situation, and I'll just have to make a judgment call each time."

April 25, 2001   Speaking to John King of CNN.

"They want the federal government controlling Social Security like it's some kind of federal program."

November 2, 2000   The presidential candidate speaking in St. Charles, Missouri. Reported by *USA Today*. (Note: Social Security **is** a federal program.)

"The American people wants a President that appeals to the angels."

August 2000   From a speech delivered at the GOP Convention.

"The federal government puts about 6% of the money up. They put about 60% of the strings, where you go to fill out paperwork. [A teacher] has to be a paperwork-filler-outer."

October 17, 2000   St. Louis, Missouri.

"If the East Timorians decide to revolt, I'm sure I'll have a statement."

June 16, 1999   As quoted in *The New York Times.*

"The Senate needs to leave enough money in the proposed budget to not only reduce all marginal rates, but to eliminate the death tax, so that people who build up assets are able to transfer them from one generation to the next, regardless of a person's race."

April 5, 2001   Washington, D.C.

PRESIDENTIAL (Mis)SPEAK

"He understands our belief in free trade. He understands I want to ensure our relationship with our most important neighbor to the north of us, Canadians, is strong."

March 3, 2000 The presidential candidate was answering a question about the Canadian Prime Minister. (The questioner was not a journalist, but rather a TV personality in Canada and the name used in the question to refer to the Prime Minister was invented—"Prime Minister Jean Poutine") Reported in *The Wall Street Journal.*

"I think what we need to do is convince people who live in the lands they live in to build the nations."

October 11, 2000 Presidential debate, Winston Salem, North Carolina.

"When I was coming up, it was a dangerous world, and you knew exactly who they were. It was us versus them, and it was clear who 'them' was. Today we are not so sure who the they are, but we know they're there."

January 21, 2000   From a speech given at Iowa Western Community College.

"Right hand up, please. Actually, right hand on your heart."

July 11, 2001   President Bush's instructions to a group of new citizens at an Ellis Island citizenship ceremony. He was leading them in the Pledge of Allegiance. Reported by *Reuters*.

Bush: "First of all, Cinco de Mayo is not the Independence Day. That's dieciseis de Septiembre."

Matthews: "What's that in English?"

Bush: "Fifteenth of September."

May 31, 2000   Dieciseis de Septiembre is September 16. Speaking on MSNBC's *Hardball With Chris Matthews.*

"We need to change that attitude about how prolific we can be with the people's money."

March 16, 2001

"Vice President mentioned Nigeria is a fledgling democracy. We have to work with Nigeria. That's an important continent."

October 11, 2000 Presidential debate, Winston-Salem, North Carolina.

"When we carry Iowa in November, it'll mean the end of four years of Clinton-Gore."

August 22, 2000 Referring to the two-term, eight-year presidency of Clinton/Gore.

" 'Oh, please don't kill me.' "

Circa 2000 The Governor's answer when asked by reporters what condemned inmate, Carla Faye Tucker, had written to him in her appeal for clemency.

"And I see Bill Buckley is here tonight—fellow Yale man. We go way back, and we have a lot in common. Bill wrote a book at Yale—I read one."

October 19, 2000 Comments made at the Al Smith Memorial Dinner in New York.

"The best way to relieve families from time is to let them keep some of their own money."

September 13, 2000 Comment made in Westminster, California.

"Diseases… such as arthritis and osteoporosis, can be less beea, beea-dilatating."

March 21, 2001

"Of all states that understands local control of schools, Iowa is such a state."

February 28, 2001   Comment made in Council Bluffs, Iowa.

"Education is not my top priority—education is my top priority."

February 27, 2001   From a budget speech in Washington, D.C.

The Very Curious Language of George W. Bush™
Volume 1

PRESIDENTIAL (Mis)SPEAK

"The most important job is not to be Governor, or First Lady in my case."

January 30, 2000 From a speech in Pella, Iowa, and quoted in the *San Antonio Express-News.*

"And the true threats of the 21st century are the ability for some rogue leader to say to the United States, to Europe, to Russia herself, to Israel, don't you dare move, don't you dare try to express your freedom, otherwise we'll blow you up."

July 20, 2001 BBC interview.

Reporter: "Do you know who the President of India is?"

Bush: "Vajpayee"

February 25, 2000 Candidate Bush's answer after requesting that a reporter quiz him on the name of India's "President." Atal Behari Vajpayee is the Prime Minister of India. Earlier in the campaign the candidate had been asked to name India's Prime Minister and had been unable to do so. (K. R. Narayanan is the President of India). Reported by *The New York Times*.

"I'm trying to protect my invest— my contributors from unscrupulous practices."

July 18, 1998 Quoted in the *Houston Chronicle*.

"It's one thing about insurance, that's a Washington term."

October 18, 2000 Comment made in St. Louis, Missouri.

PRESIDENTIAL (Mis)SPEAK

"I'm a strong candidate because I come from the baby-boomer generation, recognizing that we've got to usher in an era of responsible behavior."

April 27, 2000 Comment from an interview on *The NewsHour with Jim Lehrer.*

"A reformer with results is a conservative who has had compassionate results in the state of Texas."

February 10, 2000 Quoted by *The New York Times.*

PRESIDENTIAL (Mis)SPEAK

"The explorationists are willing to only move equipment during the winter, which means they'll be on ice roads, and remove the equipment as the ice begins to melt, so that the fragile tundra is protected."

May 18, 2001   From a speech made in Conestoga, Pennsylvania.

"I am a person who recognizes the fallacy of humans."

September 19, 2000   Comment made on TV talk show, *Oprah*.

"Look, this is a man. He's got great numbers. He talks about numbers. I'm beginning to think not only did he invent the Internet, but he invented the calculator."

October 3, 2000   First presidential debate. Boston, Massachusetts.

"[Vice President Gore will create] over 200,000 new or expanded federal programs."

October 1, 2000   The presidential candidate meant 200 new programs.

"It is not Reaganesque to support a tax plan that is Clinton in nature."

February 23, 2000   From comments made in Los Angeles and reported by *Slate* magazine.

"I look forward to seeing [Tony Blair] at Chequers. And we sat next to each other at my first EU (European Union) luncheon—NATO luncheon —anyway, at the first luncheon with leaders, I sat next to Tony."

July 20, 2001   BBC interview.

"John, we're going to get a good bill. I mean, one of the things I've learned is not to try to negotiate with you or me on national TV."

April 25, 2001 Comment made during interview with CNN's John King.

"I knew it might put him in an awkward position that we had a discussion before finality has finally happened in this presidential race."

December 2, 2000 Referring to a phone conversation with Louisiana Democratic Senator, John Breaux.

"But the true threats to stability and peace are these nations that are not very transparent, that hide behind the—that don't let people in to take a look and see what they're up to. They're very kind of authoritarian regimes. The true threat is whether or not one of these people decide, pique of anger, try to hold us hostage, ourselves; the Israelis, for example, to whom we'll defend, offer our defenses; the South Koreans."

March 13, 2001   Speaking to the media in Washington, D.C.

"Mr. Vice President, in all due respect, it is—I'm not sure—80% of the people get the death tax. I know this: 100% will get it if I'm the President."

October 17, 2000 From presidential debate in St. Louis, Missouri.

"It is incredibly presumptive for somebody who has not yet earned his party's nomination to start speculating about vice presidents."

October 22, 1999 Comment made while visiting Keene, New Hampshire.

"How do you know, if you don't measure, if you have a system that simply suckles kids through?"

February 16, 2000   Comment made in Beaufort, South Carolina.

"I made the decision to name the Justice Department building after Robert Kennedy because he's deservant."

November 20, 2001   Speaking to reporters in the Oval Office about his decision to name the Justice Department building after former U.S. Attorney General, Robert Kennedy. Aired on CNN.

"I don't know, maybe I made it up. Anyway, it's an arbo-tree-ist, somebody who knows about trees."

August 2001   Referring to the arborist who had been asked to identify trees on the President's Crawford, Texas, ranch. Quoted in *USA Today* and *Time* magazine.

PRESIDENTIAL (Mis)SPEAK

"We like living in the White House. It's a nice place to live."

August 25, 2001 Speaking to a reporter at his Crawford, Texas, ranch.

"We have struggled to not proceed, but to precede to the future of a nation's child."

November 12, 2000 Quoted in the *Journal Gazette*.

"We've got to end the process-oriented world of public schools."

March 20, 2001

"In terms of the CO_2 issue... We will not do anything that harms our economy, because, first things first, are the people who live in America."

Circa February 2001

"I'm gonna get it mixed up but they had 10,000 square foot of warehouse; now they've got hundreds of thousands of square foot of warehouse."

January 5, 2002   Referring to a corporate success story in California (the JCM Corporation). Town hall meeting in Ontario, California.

PRESIDENTIAL (Mis)SPEAK

"The only people who are going to support Russia are Russia."

October 11, 2000   Presidential debate, Winston-Salem, North Carolina.

"I flew down on the airplane today with some distinguished members of the North Carolina congressional delegation. First, a true gentleman, and somebody every time I sees him talks about North Carolina in the most glowing terms, and that's Senator Jesse Helms."

January 30, 2002   Speaking in Winston-Salem, North Carolina.

"This campaign not only hears the voices of the entrepreneurs and the farmers and the entrepreneurs, we hear the voices of those struggling to get ahead."

August 21, 2000 From a campaign stop in Des Moines, Iowa.

"The federal government ought to have maximum flexibility."

September 30, 2000 The presidential candidate was referring to "states" having flexibility in their use of education funds.

PRESIDENTIAL (Mis)SPEAK

"I can't remember any specific books."

August 26, 1999 The candidate's answer when asked by an elementary school student to name his favorite book as a child. Reported by the *Associated Press*.

"Even though we're at war, even though we're at recession, the state of our union has never been stronger."

January 30, 2002 Speaking in Winston-Salem, North Carolina, the day after giving his State of the Union speech to Congress.

"They're seeking chemical, biological, and nucular weapons."

November 6, 2001 Speaking from the White House via satellite to Central European leaders gathered in Warsaw. The President is referring to goals of the Qaeda terrorist group. Aired on ABC *Evening News*.

"And, by the way, I'm still negotiating with myself... And good Americans such as yourself are trying to get me to negotiate with myself."

March 29, 2001 White House press conference.

"I am mindful of the difference between the executive branch and the legislative branch. I assured all four of these leaders that I know the difference."

December 18, 2000 Washington, D.C. Reported by *Slate* magazine.

"You subscribe politics to it. I subscribe freedom to it."

April 6, 2000 Referring to the Elian Gonzalez negotiations in Miami, Florida. Reported by the *Associated Press.*

"I am a living example of someone who took on an issue and benefited from it."

April 25, 2001 Speaking to John King of CNN.

"[I have] ruled out no new Social Security taxes."

October 1, 2000 He was thought to mean that new Social Security taxes were ruled out. Reported by *The Washington Post.*

The Very Curious Language of George W. Bush™
Volume 1

Bush: "Can **you** name the foreign minister of Mexico?"

Reporter: "No, sir. No, sir. But I would say to that, I'm not running for President."

Bush: "I understand. I understand, but the point I say to you is, is that, you know, if what you're suggesting is, is that—what I'm suggesting to you is if you can't name the foreign minister of Mexico, therefore, you know, you're not capable of what you do. But the truth of the matter is, you're is—you are, whether you can or not."

November 4, 1999

"One of the great things about books is sometimes there are some fantastic pictures."

January 3, 2000   Quoted in *U.S. News & World Report.*

"People make suggestions on what to say all the time. I'll give you an example. I don't read what's handed to me. People say, 'Here, here's your speech,' or 'Here's an idea for a speech.' They're changed. Trust me."

March 15, 2000   Quoted in *The New York Times.*

"We just had some really good news out of Yugoslavia. I'm especially pleased that Mr. Milosevic has stepped down. That's one less Polyslavic name for me to remember."

October 19, 2000   Speaking at the Al Smith Memorial Dinner in New York.

"Every morning I wake up. And when I wake up I go to the Oval Office."

January 5, 2001   Town hall meeting in Ontario, California.

"I do not agree with this notion that somehow if I go to try to attract votes and to lead people toward a better tomorrow somehow I get subscribed to some—some doctrine gets subscribed to me."

February 13, 2000   Referring to his visit to Bob Jones University. From NBC's *Meet the Press*.

"Not over my dead body will they raise your taxes."

January 5, 2002   Referring to Democrats opposed to the administration's tax policy. Town hall meeting in Ontario, California.

"If a person doesn't have the capacity that we all want that person to have, I suspect hope is in the far distant future, if at all."

May 22, 2001   From a speech delivered to the Hispanic Scholarship Fund Institute. Washington, D.C.

Reporter: "Can you name him [the Pakistani leader]?"

Bush: "General—I can't name the general. General."

November 4, 1999

Reporter: "And the Prime Minister of India?" [can you name him?]

Bush: "The new Prime Minister of India is—no."

November 4, 1999

"You've heard Al Gore say he invented the Internet. Well, if he was so smart, why do all the addresses begin with 'W'?"

October 28, 2000

PRESIDENTIAL (Mis)SPEAK

"This is a world that is much more uncertain than the past. In the past we were certain—we were certain it was us versus the Russians in the past. We were certain, and therefore we had huge nucular arsenals aimed at each other to keep the peace. That's what we were certain of... You see, even though it's an uncertain world, we're certain of some things. We're certain that even though the 'evil empire' may have passed, evil still remains. We're certain there are people that can't stand what America stands for... We're certain there are madmen in this world, and there's terror, and there's missiles and I'm certain of this, too: I'm certain, to maintain the peace, we better have a military of high morale, and I'm certain that, under this administration, morale in the military is dangerously low."

May 31, 2000 Comments made during a campaign stop in Albuquerque, New Mexico. Reported by *The Washington Post.*

The Very Curious Language of George W. Bush™
Volume 1

"We cannot start Mitchell, the Mitchell Plan, until the cycle of violence has been crushed and broken."

June 20, 2001 Washington, D.C.

★ ★ ★ ★

"When Europe and America are divided, history tends to tragedy."

June 15, 2001

★ ★ ★ ★

"When I'm the President, we're not going to obfuscate when it comes to foreign policy."

January 7, 2000 Republican debate in New Hampshire.

★ ★ ★ ★

Bush: "I am for 'don't ask, don't tell.' This is a policy that Colin Powell thoughtfully put in place."

Reporter: "That's the Clinton policy."

Bush: "Well, if that's the Clinton policy, I support that."

August 14, 1999 Speaking on CNN.

"My education message will resignate amongst all parents."

January 19, 2000 Quoted in the *New York Post*.

PRESIDENTIAL (Mis)SPEAK

"I thought we ought to raise the age at which juveniles can have a gun."

October 18, 2000 From a speech in St. Louis, Missouri.

"If he's—the inference is that somehow he thinks slavery is a—is a noble institution, I would—I would strongly reject that assumption, that John Ashcroft is a open-minded, inclusive person."

January 14, 2001 From the *NBC Nightly News with Tom Brokaw.*

"Our nation must come together to unite."

June 4, 2001 Remark made in Tampa, Florida.

"Then I went for a run with the other dog and just walked. And I started thinking about a lot of things. I was able to—I can't remember what it was. Oh, the inaugural speech, started thinking through that."

January 22, 2001 From an interview with *U.S. News & World Report*.

"I'm hopeful. I know there is a lot of ambition in Washington, obviously. But I hope the ambitious realize that they are more likely to succeed with success as opposed to failure."

January 18, 2001 Comments made to the *Associated Press*.

"You might want to comment on that, Honorable."

July 15, 2000 Governor Bush was speaking to the New Jersey Secretary of State, the Honorable DeForest Soaries. Reported by *The Washington Post*.

"So, on behalf of a well-oiled unit of people who came together to serve something greater than themselves, congratulations."

May 31, 2001   White House ceremony honoring the University of Nebraska women's volleyball team, the 2001 NCAA Champions.

"I think we need not only to eliminate the tollbooth to the middle class, I think we should knock down the tollbooth."

February 1, 2000   From a speech in Nashua, New Hampshire. Quoted in *The New York Times*.

"… deteriate (deteriorate)… hayenous (heinous)… vented (vetted)…"

May 14, 2001 Mispronunciations committed during one informal press conference at the White House.

"First, we would not accept a treaty that would not have been ratified, nor a treaty that I thought made sense for the country."

April 24, 2001 Referring to the Kyoto Accord. From an interview published in the *Washington Post*.

"If I don't practice I am going to destroy this language."

June 12, 2001 Statement made by the President after mispronouncing the Spanish Prime Minister's name and making grammatical and pronunciation errors during an interview with Spanish TV.

The Very Curious Language of George W. Bush™
Volume 1

"Nobody needs to tell me what I believe. But I do need somebody to tell me where Kosovo is."

August 25, 1999   Quoted in *Talk*.

"There's not going to be enough people in the system to take advantage of people like me."

June 9, 2000   Referring to a possible Social Security crisis. Wilton, Connecticut.

Reporter: "Can you name the President of Chechnya?"

Bush: "No, can you?"

November 4, 1999

"There needs to be debates, like we're going through. There needs to be town hall meetings. There needs to be travel. This is a huge country."

December 16, 1999 From an appearance on CNN's *Larry King Live.*

"I want you to know that farmers are not going to be secondary thoughts to a Bush administration. They will be in the forethought of our thinking."

August 10, 2000 Salinas, California.

"One of the common denominators I have found is that expectations rise above that which is expected."

September 27, 2000 From a speech in Los Angeles, California.

"[We will] use our technology to enhance uncertainties abroad."

March 6, 2000 The President was referring to foreign threats, including terrorism. Quoted in *The New York Times*.

"The California crunch really is the result of not enough power generating plants and then not enough power to power the power of generating plants."

January 14, 2001 From an interview with *The New York Times*. (Referring to the California energy crisis.)

The Very Curious Language of George W. Bush™
Volume 1

"If I'm the President, we're going to have emergency-room care, we're going to have gag orders."

October 18, 2000 From comments in St. Louis, Missouri.

"Other Republican candidates may retort to personal attacks and negative ads."

March 24, 2000 George W. Bush fund-raising letter. Quoted in *The Washington Post*.

"We need to do what we need to do to get the bodies out of there, if they're there."

February 14, 2001 Referring to the tragic sinking of a Japanese fishing boat by a U.S. submarine near Hawaii. Reported in the *Chicago Tribune*.

"There's a huge trust. I see it all the time when people come up to me and say, 'I don't want you to let me down again.'"

October 3, 2000 Boston, Massachusetts.

"It was just inebriating what Midland [Oil Company] was all about then."

Comment made in a 1994 interview. Quoted in *First Son*, by Bill Minutaglio.

"The point is, this is a way to help inoculate me about what has come and is coming."

September 2, 2000 Referring to his campaign's anti-Gore advertising. From an interview with *The New York Times*.

PRESIDENTIAL (Mis)SPEAK

"There's no question that the minute I got elected, the storm clouds on the horizon were getting nearly directly overhead."

May 11, 2001   Washington, D.C.

"We must have the attitude that every child in America, regardless of where they're raised or how they're born, can learn."

April 18, 2001   From a speech delivered in New Britain, Connecticut.

[Mr. Gore believes the federal surplus] "is the people's money."

October 31, 2000   Meaning to say that the Vice President feels the surplus is the 'government's money.' Reported by *The New York Times.*

The Very Curious Language of George W. Bush™
Volume 1

"I think we're making progress. We understand where the power of this country lay. It lays in the hearts and souls of Americans. It must lay in our pocketbooks. It lays in the willingness for people to work hard. But as importantly, it lays in the fact that we've got citizens from all walks of life, all political parties, that are willing to say, I want to love my neighbor."

April 11, 2001   From a speech at the Concord Middle School in Concord, North Carolina.

PRESIDENTIAL (Mis)SPEAK

"I think if you know what you believe, it makes it a lot easier to answer questions. I can't answer your question."

October 4, 2000 Speaking in Reynoldsburg, Ohio.

"Presidents, whether things are good or bad, get the blame. I understand that."

May 11, 2001 Washington, D.C.

"Sitting down and reading a 500-page book on public policy or philosophy or something."

September, 1999 The presidential candidate's answer when asked by an interviewer to name something he was not very good at. Quoted in *Talk* magazine.

"I think we ought to have high—high standards and set by—by agencies that rely upon science, not by what may feel good or what sound good."

January 15, 2000   From Republican debate in Des Moines, Iowa.

"My opponent seems to think that Social Security is a federal program. I believe that money is yours and you should be able to invest it yourself."

October 17, 2000   Third presidential debate. St. Louis, Missouri. (Note: Social Security **is** a federal program.)

PRESIDENTIAL (Mis)SPEAK

"I regret that a private comment I made to the vice presidential candidate made it through the public airways."

September 5, 2000 Alluding to an unfavorable comment (unpublishable in this calendar) he had made about a certain reporter. Allentown, Pennsylvania.

"You teach a child to read, and he or her will be able to pass a literacy test."

February 21, 2001 From a speech delivered in Townsend, Tennessee. Reported by *The New Republic* (March 5, 2001 issue).

"When I put my hand on the Bible, I will swear to not—to uphold the laws of the land."

October 27, 2000 Toledo, Ohio.

"We don't believe in planners and deciders making the decisions on behalf of Americans."

September 6, 2000 From a speech delivered in Scranton, Pennsylvania.

"My view is that state law reigns supreme when it comes to the Indians, whether it be gambling or any other issue."

November 4, 1999 The Texas Governor was forgetting that U.S. Government treaties with Native Americans always take precedence over state laws.

"I'm confident people are coming together. And the reason I believe this is because our party is united."

July 19, 2000 From Fox TV's *Special Report With Brit Hume*.

The Very Curious Language of George W. Bush™
Volume 1

"I'm a uniter, not a divider. That means when it comes time to sew up your chest cavity, we use stitches as opposed to opening it up."

March 2, 2000 On CBS's *Late Show with David Letterman.* The late night talk show host had recently undergone open heart surgery.

"I did denounce it. I de—I denounced it. I denounced interracial dating. I denounced anti-Catholic bigacy—bigotry."

February 25, 2000 The candidate responding to criticism that he visited Bob Jones University.

"We're ending deadlock and drift and making our system on behalf of the American people."

August 3, 2001 Addressing reporters at the White House.

"I don't remember debates. I don't think we spent a lot of time debating it. Maybe we did, but I don't remember."

July 27, 1999 Referring to whether he had discussions about the Vietnam War while an undergraduate at Yale University. Reported by *The Washington Post*.

"America is not ready to overturn Roe v. Wade because America's hearts are not right."

March 10, 1999

"It's amazing to be interested in history and living—making history. It's an interesting coincidence."

February 5, 1999   From a C-Span interview and as quoted in the *Jewish World Review.*

"Well, we all make mistakes. I've been known to mangle a syl-lab'-ble or two myself, you know."

October 11, 2000   Second presidential debate. Winston-Salem, North Carolina.

"Oh, I thought you said 'some band.' The Taliban in Afghanistan! Absolutely—repressive."

Circa June 2000   After seeming confused when asked a question about the Taliban, Governor Bush responded after being prompted by the reporter, "Repression of women in Afghanistan?"

"You'll be in a world in which fits into my philosophy. You know, the harder work—the harder you work, the more you can keep. That's the American way."

October 17, 2000   Third presidential debate in St. Louis, Missouri.

"As far as the legal hassling and wrangling and posturing in Florida, I would suggest you talk to our team in Florida led by Jim Baker."

November 30, 2000   Statement by the candidate from Crawford, Texas.

"I would have my Secretary of Treasury be in touch with the financial centers not only here but at home."

October 3, 2000 First presidential debate in Boston, Massachusetts. The candidate was responding to a question about how he would react to a world-wide financial crisis.

"I think he needs to stand up and say, if he thought the President were wrong on policy and issues, he ought to say where."

August 11, 2000 Referring to Al Gore and Bill Clinton. From an interview with the *Associated Press*.

"I think anybody who doesn't think I'm smart enough to handle the job is underestimating."

April 3, 2000 As reported in *U.S. News & World Report*.

ACKNOWLEDGMENTS

First of all, I wish to thank my family members who never lost faith in either this project or me, even after the tragic events of September 11, 2001, becalmed our efforts for an entire year. To my sister Nancy, her husband Mac, and my brother Art, far away in Thailand — your support and loyalty were sustaining and I'll be forever grateful.

To my wife, Joni, and our six wonderful and beautiful girls — I love you all the more for having so patiently put up with the chaos and uncertainty this project brought to our lives. You are all deserving of more calm and tranquil times.

To my parents, who always believed in their children and stood solidly by each of us as we grew and took on projects and careers. That unflinching support laid a foundation which gave me the confidence to carry forward with this book despite the uncertainty brought on by terrorist attacks, war, and unusually high presidential approval ratings.

A very special thanks goes to the people at Outland who championed this undertaking from its earliest inception. Without your belief in the concept, this book (and the volumes to follow) as well as the annual Bush Desk Calendar series would never have been realized. Specifically, I would like to thank Joyce Oliveri, and Will and Barbara McGrath. Joyce, I know you took a chance and I'm so grateful. Will, looking back through the haze of the last year, there is some faint memory that this book was your idea...

Further thanks goes to the people at HumanDesign. Mary, thank you so much for your exquisite attention to detail. And to David Carlson, this book and the President Bush calendar series all bear your masterful imprint. It was such a pleasure working with you. Hopefully, though I'm not sure, you feel the same.

I would like to express appreciation to everyone at Banta Book Group for helping me to learn my way. Specifically, many thanks to Rence Rosenow, Bob Christopher, Sue Vandewalle, and Jim Martin.

To my proofreader, Donna Himelfarb, thanks for being at the ready on such short notice. Any and all mistakes should be referred to Donna. I'm off the hook!

I am grateful to my old high school buddy, John Birk, for dispensing advice so willingly. Thanks to another high school pal, Jeff Sagansky, for being there and willing to help out after so many years. Thanks also to my fellow wrestling coach, Tim Green, for leading me to the epicenter of the world of "publishers' representatives" — though he's most likely too busy to remember.

For his somewhat startling pronouncement found on the back cover of this book, special thanks to Dr. Scott Anderson. And furthermore Scott, I so very much appreciate your long-standing encouragement.

Additional thanks goes to Ken Casarsa and his whole crew at MRA for helping to make the 2003 George W. Bush Desk Calendar such a success. We'll never know exactly how key your publicity campaign was, but surely it helped put sales over the top.

Finally, I would like to acknowledge those people who still understand that the unrestrained expression of myriad points of view is not somehow antithetical to the concepts of freedom and patriotism, but rather, quite the opposite.

2004 Desk Calendar of Presidential (Mis)Speak
Completely Updated
All New Quotes

Available wherever books and calendars are sold

and at

www.bushcalendar.com

Outland Books

Skaneateles, New York